Journey to the Sun

Also by Cadeyn McLellan

The Primordial Mind
Exodus

Copyright information

Quotations taken from;
- *King James Bible*. (1973). Holman Bible Publishers. (Original work published 1611)
- Alighieri, D. (2010). *The Divine Comedy*. Penguin Books. (Original work published 1321)

All works quoted are in the public domain.

Cover art by Stefano B. Edied by Michael Martin. Artist photo taken by Bek Stokes. Published and distributed through Ingram Spark.

Copyright © 2025 by Cadeyn McLellan. All rights reserved. No portion of this book may be reproduced in any form without written permission from the publisher or author, except as permitted by U.S. copyright law.

ISBN: 978-1-7640159-0-5 First Edition Hardback.

Volume 1: Journey to the Sun

For my wife, Amelia.

Introduction

I began to write poetry when I was engaged to be married, and predictably, most of it was awful. But one poem, "The Hourglass," I worked and worked until I realized I had something, like a flame out of two sticks. Now ten years on, coinciding with the birth of my son Ransom, I am publishing my poetry.

Looking at the timing of things, I now see how my wife guided me in this journey- mostly through her patience and kindness. My wife has always been a selfless encourager of others.

Volume 1
Journey to the Sun

Volume 1: Journey to the Sun

Chapter 1: In Endless Sea

1. Child of Atlantis — 2
2. Mermaids — 4

Chapter 2: Jurassic Coast

3. Attenborough and the Sea Dragon — 8
4. The Ocean's Daughter — 9

Chapter 3: Garden of Memory

5. Memory — 12
6. Love Before Eve — 18
7. Nature Falls — 20

Chapter 4: Light Beyond the Sea

8. The Holy Mountain — 26
9. Fibonacci — 29
10. Fading Embers — 32
11. Love — 33

Chapter 5: Roaming with Celestials

12. The Hourglass — 36

In Endless Sea

Child of Atlantis
Innocence

Gazing out at the abyss,
Where once there rose fair Atlantis:
An island of mysteries,
Existing free of tragedy;
All her shores in bounty blessed,
In hopefulness and timelessness.
Nights in dripping moon light run
And days laden with sweat of sun;
Colours to the world now lost,
In relics past the weight of cost.
Youths in song would dance and twirl
Along her streets aglow in pearl.
Vigour and in valour bound,
Assurance of our folklore found.
In the strength of battlements,
Which never sung in song lament
Wrapped up in sweet turquoise seas,
Without Poseidon's agony:
Citizens of innocence,
To the outside's experience;
Seasons I had thought would last,
In vernal days that never pass.
Yet these riches fade away,
In memory's unfaithful sway.
And the sight that now remains,
Is of the downfall and the pain.
Inside splashing crashing swells
That drowned my precious citadel.
Innocence was shed from me
As drinking full the wrath of sea.

Child of Atlantis
Experience

Now I sing in eulogy,
Where once I sang of victory:
Crying out into the mist,
Relinquish me in ocean hiss.
Yet my words won't do such things,
And only sorrow do they bring.
Eyes of grey and sunken realms,
And memory lies at my helm,
Offering to me a kiss,
Of places lost which I so miss.
Memory's sweet melodies,
An ecstasy in brevity.
Sirens circle ceaselessly,
With songs of tempting treachery
Dragging me into the depths,
Where my Atlantis dwells in death.
Yet although I long for home,
I cannot claim her as my own.
For to me she was a gift,
Her gardens hung I did not lift;
I laid not her palisades,
Nor by my hands her paths were paved.
To Atlantis debt is owed,
For all that she to me bestowed.
So from memory I build
A place my children now to fill.
So they may have memory
To fill them with her jubilee.
And so, vicariously,
Atlantis is restored to me.

Mermaids

1

In the swell from shore I saw
A myriad of mermaids, happy eyes:
Majesty and mystery unmarred,
In each character and nature unique:
Beautiful daughters,
Wrapped in their mother's waters,
Floating free in endless sea.
Mind and body, humanity,
Their kingdom of corals unblemished.
And I gazed, innocent as they,
Such beauty in the unknown, choice to be shown
Their scales reflecting
Sunlight and sea spray redirecting.
And the sun, the sun, clear and warm,
Shadowless and full,
Giving all things their true form.
Dressed in the turquoise shallows,
There was an honesty in sight,
The protection of love and light.
And they dove beneath the waves;
My contented child eyes, still wise,
Farewelled them with a wave.

Mermaids

2

Through the moonlight led by adult eyes
To the dreamscape neon town,
Beguiling senses, vanquished guilt,
Moon shadowing dirty shallows,
I gazed into the glazed windows
Saw through the glass the mermaids,
Lay quantified, cauterised, opiate eyed,
Character banished; body famished,
Dissected, pinned open, broken.
Displayed, hidden from the light of day,
Branded name and number numb.
Their meat lay on tables,
Feasted on by predators.
Bloodshot eyes watch from pig troughs:
Everything seen, Nothing real.
Lies answer mysteries, desecrating majesty.
Love bottled in syringes,
Veins pulsate and medicate,
Injecting mermaid blood, Venus intravenous.
Their life the sacrifice for desire's vice:
Lust liquidated as love is lost.

Jurassic Coast

Attenborough and the Sea Dragon

A dragon descends the Jurassic deep,
Chaotic jaws where life and death combine.
When killing makes some sand his deathly keep,
His tooth and rib in silt so black enshrine.

In love, man etches stone from dragon bone;
In lust, man leaks the dragon blood to sea.
Are dragons here to paint or overthrow?
In love and lust our hearts dividing plea.

Jurassic Coast, eternity in time:
So momentary her stewards are we.
For chaos subdued is something divine,
Our stony hearts need pruning to be free.

To man, these fossils, the reflection clear;
To chaos, or beauty, our choice to steer.

The Ocean's Daughter

The shore beheld his destined love,
Her figure wrapped in blessed grace.
The sea and sun formed high above,
And created in warmest place.

Awaiting in my lonely dunes,
Illuminated by the moon,
To marry her within the sun,
Where sand and ocean become one.

The ocean took up precious form,
All nature in her form was spanned.
In water eyes and beauty warm,
The daughter of the ocean's hands.

Now lying low my old sand dunes,
In light of the now fading moon,
And in the rising of the sun,
Where sand and ocean can be one.

In breaking waves her beating heart,
Drags my shoreline out to sea.
My solitude broken apart,
As, overwhelmed, she married me.

Now water fills my old sand dunes,
Behind me now are night and moon.
For marriage is the rising sun,
Where sand and ocean became one.

Garden of Memory

Memory

"He has also set eternity in the human heart."

1

Memory.
Stars which burn
And in twinkling turn.
Memory.
Glowing Xibalba spiralling
Death and rebirth her eternal ring.
Cleaving to the fabric of her shroud
Interweaving those great cosmic clouds.
Memory.
Starlight itself is a beautiful dance of eulogy,
For countless dead stars are still shining trajectories.
We their terrestrial progeny bask in their passing beauty
Even our own sun lives in eight minutes of memory.
Memory.
Gazing upwards at their luminous dance
We can enter their heavenly trance.
Hearts beat like cosmic storms,
We are of stardust formed.
Memory.

Memory

2

Memory.
A little calf runs
An elephant's beloved son.
Memory.
Leads the matriarch into the graveyard
The dark earth where ancestors stand guard.
As elder elephants delicately stroke the bones,
Trunks smoothing them like water over stones.
Memory.
The little boy stroking his grandmother's vertebrae
A garden of memory forming in his mind like clay.
As elephant tears dash the dry savannah sand
In growing awareness of his mortal span.
Memory.
Leads the herd in days unnumbered
By a touch of eternity encumbered.
For memory is family,
Grief and finality.
Memory.

Memory

3

Memory.
Fossils of ancient trees
Fills the dunes of modern seas.
Memory.
Turns bone to stone in loving splendour
Preserving amber moments cruel and tender.
From an ancient coelacanth to a raptor embryo,
The memory of the earth to us has been bestowed.
Memory.
Filling a young child up with enchanted fascination
To gaze amazed upon distant and primal creation
Before men from stardust found their birth
Laid deep in the foundations of earth.
Memory.
Ancient leviathans now long lost,
Their forms in slate embossed.
Life enshrined in fossils,
Small and colossal.
Memory.

Memory

4

Memory.
In a camera flash
And a photograph cache.
Memory.
Lens gleaning with a happy child
The iridescent sheen of nostalgia's smile.
And we, adults, obsessively render ourselves
Forever happy; while into pain our cameras never delve.
Memory.
Bursting forth from the depths of lament and agony,
Over our pleasure and pain she stands peremptory.
She is so much more than a flash of retina burn;
She is so much harder from which to turn.
Memory.
As the negatives in a dark room adjust,
Memory informs and conforms us.
In happy and sad visage
We bear her image.
Memory.

Memory

5

Memory.
Casting atomic shadows
Swallowed in the undertow.
Memory.
The red sun rises heavy in anguish
Over countless little children vanquished.
Nagasaki painted crimson in dawning grief
As Hiroshima waylaid in sorrow without relief.
Memory.
For even down here when the form is not retained
Our mosaic of memory, here, shall forever remain
As the dawn rolls the nuclear tides slowly back
And our grieving half-lives fade to black.
Memory.
There in the flash and here in the end
Progeny left with this one friend.
In a world ripped apart,
She fills the heart.
Memory.

Memory

6

Memory.
Moves eternally
The splashing sea.
Memory.
Gentle ripples and destructive tides
That shape and move the coastal seaside.
And we, in our humanity, are sand to its call
As she forms channels and sandcastles of us all.
Memory.
That hews us upwards from the ocean floor
And carries us to our place in the shore.
Water like a spirit moving ceaselessly
Surrounding us all with memory.
Memory.
Our beautiful Atlantean bride
Where she forever resides
Inside the heart of man
Making stars of sand.
Memory.

Love Before Eve

1

The first day my eyes opened; her light green and unbroken.
That first taste of love which teemed and blossoming in her streams.
She was such a multitude; my first love in solitude.
And I chased her through the trees, and she blessed me with her heart.

2

Her heart was a garden green, where the fig and wasp convene.
Her gifts of flower and fruit, magnolia's twisting roots.
I lie safe within her walls blanketed by mane and shawl.
And I was like a child, and like a mother she stood.

3

She stood in the rising Sun; our hands were entwined as one.
Through her lilies and willows; love without thorn or shadow,
Dispersing seeds from my palms; as her robins sang me psalms.
I could not encapsulate; her for all her artistry.

4

Her artistry vast as sea; infinite variety.
Each to their kind were woven in fear and wonder chosen:
Some which resonate the deep; others which clamber the peaks.
So I gave her many names, for she had many faces.

5

Many faces taking form like lyrebird song conformed.
Through her feathers soft and curled to my hands gently unfurled.
Our social union so stirred; as orchids to hummingbirds.
And she grew two trees for me; I took to be wedding rings.

6

Wedding rings and life endless; calling me to transcendence.
From a hundred million years; taught me to behold and fear.
In this moment of wonder; like frogs in evening thunder.
And she wrought tempest and calm, and to shore I swam the waves.

Love Before Eve

7

The waves splashing chaotic; beautiful and erotic.
Alligator vibrations; and albatross migrations,
Yet I still embryonic, happy in love platonic.
She as earth was fully grown; I a virgin to love songs.

8

Loves songs may last but a day, as Mayflies in fading rays.
No regrets of coming night; time has no bearing on flight.
Meaning gives longevity; to seconds and centuries.
She feathered and serpentine; and I flew with her on wings.

9

On wings through meadows wondered; yet as she danced I pondered.
She in all her beauty burst had not satisfied my thirst.
In her faces I found none; by which my heart was undone.
For she was a different kind; and I tired of our dance.

10

Our dance in the rising morn; filled me with names to adorn.
Yet solitude of twilight; doubting her in coming night.
Of her fruits I wanted more; some different taste to explore.
Yet she offered nothing new; and I precluded my heart.

11

My heart and sun going down; she in her nocturnal gown;
I was surrounded alone; in her most beautiful home.
By an ethereal sleep; taken down into the deep.
As she stood by my side; and I longed for someone new.

12

Someone new of shapes unknown; curves and contours bone of bone;
A similar symmetry; to the heart beating in me.
And I awoke to the Eve; flesh of my flesh to receive.
I was lost to ecstasy; and she stood on in nightfall.

Nature Falls
Part 1: Birth

Ancient days, in the rays of the sun rising new,
Garden walls covered all that in harmony grew.
Her beauty, our duty: ever work and subdue:
Mother Earth, and her worth in innocence we knew.
In great looms, flowers bloomed, majestic green and blue:
Creatures named, life inflamed by lost colours imbued.

Love to love from above in the Divine order;
Hierarchy, set us free in our garden borders.
And Mother, though lower, had man as her worker
For a time, as designed we must have adored her.
Man's nurture, of nature life upon God's arbours,
And man stood, in days good in the times now former.

Seas and streams, waters team with fish beyond number,
And the land, worked by man, bloomed in perfect summer.
In endless dependence we were kept from hunger;
And safely and carefree in Mother's arms slumbered.
The union of human and earth in days younger
Was heaven, in seven waves of warmest wonder.

Nature Falls
Part 2: Death

Yet slithered and whispered temptation's dark demands;
Such questions, suggestions: resistance did not stand.
Constricting, insisting: cold and soothing command.
So the bride, without guide in solitude was damned.
All alone, overthrown, Eve stood with fruit in hand;
Then the shame and the blame and cursed was Mother's land.

Then we weaved those fig leaves into our shameful shawl.
Mankind's curse, life inverse: now in the dust we crawl.
Paradise paid the price for mankind's ugly fall;
Frustration, creation given to desert sprawl.
Mother cries, beauty dies and the thorns take it all;
Mother wept, and was swept in the dawning nightfall.

Mother's bones built our throne and made our vulgar crowns.
Mother's seas, and their keys under man's lust was drowned.
Mother's glades, cut by blades, fuels the inferno towns.
Nature cries through her skies with thundering resound.
She laments the torment of her wilds now bound;
So afraid and betrayed, her creatures make no sound.

Nature Falls
Part 3: Rebirth

Though accursed and in thirst, our Mother stands sublime;
Leaves and root, buds and fruit still bloom in seasons' time.
Trees blushing and flushing inside the harvest rhyme;
In spring warm, petals form each to their kind assigned.
Eden's seeds still proceed to bloom colour divine;
Springtime gain, summer stain ascending to decline.

In her groans, murmured moans: she sings her prophecies
Whispering of the spring that lasts eternity.
Chaos stills, peace fulfils and no more is the sea.
The wild and child dwell without enmity.
And her lands, by our hands fill with ancient beauty,
Unhidden, forgiven, heavenly ecstasy.

There will bloom from a tomb the lyrics of new law,
Eulogy, chancing key to strings where joy does pour.
And the waste interlaced with blood is made no more,
Dawning sun, time undone, putting an end to war.
Days vernal, eternal, embraced by pristine shores:
There mankind, one in mind, and Mother's love restores.

Light Beyond the Sea

The Holy Mountain
Part I: Coexistence

We climb a Holy Mountain, wise men say,
Arising from the navel of the earth.
And every man must climb by his own way,
From cradle to the sky our death and birth.

Our pathways lifting up in eulogy,
And in our twists and turns our pathways merge.
Within the longitude of history,
Where great sherpas are calling to converge.

Muhammad marching meek and merciful,
And Jesus small and white in Mary's arms;
The Higgs and Boson Buddha Particle
In Coexistence; without any harm.

And chanting "All are holy; All are one,
Our pathway's stairway upwards to the sun."

The Holy Mountain
Part II: Stairway to Heaven

On one such pathway long since overgrown,
Where once serpents and monoliths were laid;
By heat of the Aztecan Sun was thrown,
And fierce her guards, obsidian their blades.

The Holy Mountain climbed by slave and priest,
As feathered king a-chant in ecstasy
Awaiting for a fount of blood release
As slaves dragged up the stairs in agony.

The Stairway up to Heaven painted red,
As ribs are split the mount is filled with blood.
By death the navel of the earth is fed,
With genocidal pain to fuel the flood.

If paths are equal, slave and priest are one;
And equal in their climb towards the Sun.

The Holy Mountain
Part III: Inferno and Paradiso

A mountain there is which we all must climb
In our dualistic days beneath the sun.
If all our paths are equally divine,
In evil only can they be as one.

In golden opulence of Vatican,
Religion paved in dark and shameful lust.
The Mountain homes no Good Samaritans,
Jerusalem whose beggars eat the dust.

If anything is holy it be this:
Inferno couples Paradiso.
For without one the other can't exist,
For both of which the human heart does know.

By man is the Unholy Mountain stained;
The judgement of the Sun our climb attains.

Fibonacci

1

Birth
Dawn
The sun
Circles me
In ascendency
Rising neuroplasticity
Spiraling swiftly through trees with boundless energy
Lotus patterns dance around me
Cone shell galaxies
Within me
Until
Night
Came

2

Pain
Death
To me
Oddities
Undertowed by seas
Pursuing my youth's ecstasy
Fibonacci parabolas me to agony
My folly birthing misery
Bones shatteringly
Show to me
My life
Death
Loss

Fibonacci

3
Life
Death
Cycles
Endlessly
Through time ceaselessly
Bound we are to Fibonacci
Clumsy ships in the sea writhing tempestuously
Eden's tree and eternity
To humanity
Death and sting
Within
Us
All

4
Death
Rose
In waves
Angrily
Claiming family
Mournfully I read eulogy
History told insufficiently through memory
Grief spread out like the canopy
Of a willow tree
Gravity
In death
Bound
Me

Fibonacci

5

In
Death
Consumed
Wrapping me
In mortality
Bound to fallen Fibonacci
By death my quintessence seemingly slain gracelessly
Memory seems like vanity
To my progeny
By the sea
In death
Mourn
Me

6

Yet
I
Now past
Angry seas
See Fibonacci
As it was intended to be
Not forever spiraling back to descendency
But resurrecting to eternity in heavenly quintessence beyond the sea
And I reformed of divinities perfect memory walk free of eulogy
into the dawning of Fibonacci's ascendancy

Fading Embers

An elegy for Eddie Philips

The last embers of fading light
Ebbing into the coldest night.
Shadows climbing through the amber,
Clawing through in clumsy clamber
As sparks once countless fly alone,
And ashes take the flaming throne
Like last of autumns falling leaves,
That unto life no longer cleave,
To strength of life which once did burn,
Now turn to death and dust return.

And yet among the flickering,
There lies a light still whispering.
Beneath the leaves a flower blooms,
Ascending up through Autumn's tomb.
"Know the truth, it will set you free,"
Says the eternal flame to me.
And as I strain to hear the voice,
That before death can still rejoice
There for one precious moment see,
A sea-less land of majesty.

A peaceful smile in cancer's grip;
To sleep those soft eyelids now slip.
Those withered bones still beautiful,
Purified in the crucible,
Transcending beyond space and time,
By the monitors beep and whine.
Yet I in tears no words to find,
A mourning child left behind.
As the leaf journeys from the tree,
And enters light beyond the sea.

Love

1

The stars shimmering, shifting, the cosmos infinitely lifting,
Solar flares alive and breathing.
The Godform of the ancient prayers:
Eternal genesis.
Countless, boundless, unreachable: the endless stars of heaven's table.
Light immense, unquenchable in power, grace and gravity,
From before the foundations of the earth.
And you
Grains of sand, microbes of the cosmos,
Stand humbled under the weight of the night sky.

2

Streetlights glimmering and flickering in sick amber blistering.
The hum of electricity radiates,
Light contained and isolate.
Primeval fire quantified,
Primordial glow demystified.
Cave dwellings cauterised
With neon trivialities.
As impersonation pollutes and pulsates,
The star lit night dilutes,
Barely lifting the murky gloom of the blinking cityscape.
Light was never our creation;
We but formed a sickly imitation.

Roaming with Celestials

The Hourglass
Part I

1
Upward gazed my child eyes
Towards the light that paints the skies.
Movements of celestials,
In the endless night potential.
There Orion, belt and bow
Traversing high like sailing snow.
Neptune's sea quakes violently
As Venus spins erotically.
Mars by night in endless war,
A ravaging he can't restore.
Every moon and starlit sphere
The beauty of the atmosphere.
Yet majestic as they are,
Unchanging is the walk of stars.
From the east unto the west,
Never from that path digress.
Ceaselessly Mars fights the night,
And yet his foes restored by light.
Venus beds the same lovers,
Every night like every other.

The Hourglass
Part I

2
"Did you dance in ages past
Before you lost your sail and mast?
Ancient pathways never new,
How did time come to enslave you?"
For the stars I sang lament,
And yet my song made no ascent.
For there was some entity,
Stood above in ascendency:
Gravity of blackened form,
Like some black elemental storm.
On our hearts is still graven,
Binding stars to subjugation.
What force binds eternity
Chaining stars to infirmity
Keeping the material
From roaming with celestials?
Time brought down my adult eyes,
Desert ground so desolate dry.
Putting sobered feet forward,
With my eyes no longer upward.

The Hourglass
Part I

3
Wondering through desert dunes,
Time measured up by sun and moon.
Roaming in my own reason,
Under shifting stars and seasons.
Sand before me like a sea,
Without a path was my journey.
No birdsong or human sound
Our planet is to silence bound.
Future I cannot forecast,
Nor can recall the slipping past.
I have nothing but today
Inside the sun's most blinding rays.
For man there is no freedom
Inside this desolate kingdom.
And at times I still lament,
For night brings disillusionment
Questioning the slavery
That slithers through the galaxy.
Questions go without answer,
No cure for this black cancer.

The Hourglass
Part I

4
Fruitless searching for escape
Through countless forsaken landscapes.
Night and dawn again exchanged,
Yet something in the light was strange:
A broken colour spectrum,
And within my own reflection.
Rising up a pane of glass;
In height and width of endless vast.
Covering the earth and sky,
In strength too great to be defied.
Standing at the great divide,
Eternity on the outside,
Taunted by the sight beyond,
The window of a man in bonds.
Prison bars of cosmic weight:
The world within its magistrate.
Vanity! O vanity!
Is the belief that we are free
Here inside this dark confine,
Just prisoners of death and time.

The Hourglass
Part I

5
With my hand upon the glass,
I gazed beyond: a world so vast.
As every constellation
Gazed upon my isolation,
Stars bound in their timeless glow:
But through this wall I cannot go.
Once again my eyes looked down
Upon the desert's shifting ground.
Watching as the desert moved,
My form was pulled and mind confused,
Caught inside the tide's constraints,
Which swept across the desert plains.
Carried by the current's reigns,
My form was just another grain.
By sand dunes all crumbling,
I faced a truth so humbling.
Enslaved to mortality,
Makes equal all humanity.
Sand are we the human race,
For those outside of time and space.

The Hourglass
Part I

6
Under time my bones they groan,
And by their weight was downwards thrown:
Forced onward by gravity,
Along with all humanity;
Dragged past the Wonder of Rhodes,
Who tumbled into song and ode.
All that I can do is peer
To where this cursed current veers
Until I see with my eyes
The current's deep and dark demise.
There at the reverse of birth,
An opening within the earth.
Here Prometheus in chains,
Below the eagle of his pain.
Soon I face that dark abyss;
Oncoming death I can't resist.
Dragged unto one destiny:
For prisoners are never free.
Then wisdom struck me at last,
This world is just an hourglass!

The Hourglass
Part I

7
Hurtling to the great unknown,
The nature of the world was shown.
This current: the reaper's hands.
Death always stalking these wastelands,
Reaching from that dark fissure
Where all life flows like a river.
Yet of water is not made,
For we the sand make its cascade.
Time and death make us all fall
In that time who will save us all?
Life above and death below,
Down in mortality we flow.
No weapon nor high tower,
No muscle or human power
That can stand that mighty tide;
No refuge under which to hide.
There, the whirlpool and abyss,
That helplessly we all witness.
Death our greatest enemy,
And mankind's only certainty.

The Hourglass
Part I

8
Blossoming like leaves in spring
As up our social bowers swing,
While in youth our bodies rise,
And death seems further than the skies.
Still time stabs us like a thorn,
For none escape that rolling dawn:
Even the most ancient trees,
Who chronicle the centuries,
In the end are laid to waste
When time through them is interlaced.
Every flower withers dark,
And age has every creature marked.
For we are the realm of man,
Clothed and bound in mortal span.
We are but the sand and dust,
That to the jaws of time are thrust,
Trapped inside the ever tide,
All hurtling down that final slide.
When from life to death we pass
To the base of the hourglass.

The Hourglass
Part I

9
All the things that mankind gave
To make a world so new and brave:
Culture and society,
On marble walls and tapestries.
Travelling to distant crags,
With speeches planting bloody flags:
Cities and our temple shrines,
In their ornate and rich design.
Like new life in labour pains,
Believing that the world could change.
And yet still death and disease
Were never cured or appeased;
For although some words remain
After their speaker has been slain,
From his words his children stray:
The works of man all slip away.
Statues crumble cities fall:
The conquerors they burnt it all.
Brave new world she rips apart,
Like vessels of a sickly heart.

The Hourglass
Part I

10
The depths of humanity
I saw inside of slavery:
Sandcastles of royalty,
The food chain called the hierarchy;
Tattooed barcodes and despair,
Blood washing down the temple stairs.
By a tyrant's cold commands,
Or by the bloody gods' demands:
People moved up like cattle,
Quetzalcoatl's dark steeple.
Chanting crowd in drum and shout,
As hearts are torn on temple mount.
Dark symbols and feathered priest.
Some in chains others hold release.
Oh! But darkest irony,
For all are yoked to slavery.
In less than the blink of eyes,
This hourglass will watch them die.
In this life is no freedom
From any spectrum of kingdom.

The Hourglass
Part I

11
Knowing that I was to die,
I looked again unto the skies,
Crying out for an escape,
From that dark pit which lay agape.
"Take me out through transcendence
To timelessness from present tense
Into the eternal realms,
Inside Orion's starlit helm."
Yet the light remained silent,
Refusing me, saving ascent.
Ancient chains still bind me down:
Prometheus ever aground.
Thrice I turned from the sunlight,
Which brings the day forth from the night,
Knowing no escape would come
And life was soon to be undone.
I can see eternity,
Yet touch it not from slavery.
There is no escape from time;
No transcendental redesign.

The Hourglass
Part I

12
To my eyes a vision came
Before freedom had lost our claim.
Past and future: they were one
Before our banishment begun.
Sand in perfect mirror form,
Before the thistles and the thorns.
Timelessness once married us,
A great marriage which turned to lust.
Our true lover hid away,
And time, our mistress, came to stay.
Mirror shattered back to sand,
This hourglass a banished land.
Then my eyes returned to me,
And fear, oh fear, what I did see!
In my dread I cried "Behold!"
The darkness which had been foretold.
With my naked eyes I saw
The deep abyss of ancient law.
On the edge of life and death
I drew and held my final breath.

The Hourglass
Part I

13
Thrown onward, hopeless screaming,
On the edge my soul was leaning.
Helpless tried to hold my ground:
The cries of death the loudest sound.
Futile against the pull,
Until I drink the cup in full.
Death! O Death! His hand on me,
My soul cried out "Please set me free!"
Only seconds left in life
Before I face the reaper's scythe.
All of my bones splintering,
All mortal strength now withering.
Choking for no air was left,
Trying to draw my final breath.
I could hear my heart pounding,
Until O Fear! it stopped sounding.
All my strength was broken:
I fell into the vast open.
Falling out of life and light,
Into the world of dawning night.

The Hourglass
Part I

14
There I lay, my body slain,
With Death himself inside my veins.
My cycle of time complete,
The lay of man finds its defeat.
Now I stood in endless days
Of truly dark and lonesome stay.
This is not eternity,
For time still owns this agony.
Man so weak diminishes,
And jackals pull the vestiges.
Here upon the River Styx,
Eternity fully eclipsed.
In life we could turn and gaze,
To timelessness from passing days.
Now in death we all are blind,
For by new walls our eyes confined.
The base of the hourglass:
A carven wall of wood and brass.
In this prison of endless time,
To us no window is assigned.

The Hourglass
Part I

15
Wandering the labyrinth maze,
As Theseus in ancient days.
Searching for the centre dark,
Yet there found no beast or mark.
Just a mirror deathly born,
And there I saw my tapered horns:
Theseus and Minotaur,
One and the same on Hades' shore.
Once Grendel and Beowulf fought,
When Grendel's arm from him was wrought.
Grendel slain on legend's page,
And so was lit the mother's rage.
In the catacombs untraced,
There Beowulf went to lay to waste.
Mother of the evil one,
That her bloodline could be undone.
Yet when dragon-fire came,
Igniting Beowulf's pyre flames.
Here Beowulf and Grendel dwell;
Inside Hades they share a cell.

The Hourglass
Part I

16
Isolated and at war,
Like castaways on foreign shores;
Following the adult's ways,
Morality still fell away.
Blood staining upon the ground,
As all around the screams resound.
Head of pig against the sky,
For here our darkened nature lies.
Without rescue here to save,
Our souls the landscape we must brave.
Wondering and murdering,
By tribal drums our demons sing
As the darker side we feed,
As wood now filled by centipedes.
In the dark we have no sight,
And from our hands there is no light.
For when we are left alone,
The seeds of light no longer sown,
Trapped in night so far from day,
We spend all time as castaways.

The Hourglass
Part I

17
Over all humanity
The hourglass has victory.
In the dark we blindly grope:
The only light, the great false hope.
From that portal where we fell:
A joke from which no laughter swells.
Such a cruel and twisted sight
For those who dwell in ever-night.
Light which is our one escape,
From Hades' desolate landscape.
Yet no soul makes the ascent;
In ashes men lay in lament.
From above no one to call,
For only down does mankind fall.
Like a bird of broken wing
Who hears the wind so sweetly sing.
In the hope that we arise
Is where our souls truly demise.
"Human race so born to fly,"
These words are just a twisted lie.

The Hourglass
Part I

18
Gazing full of agony
As passing time consuming me;
Witnessing the human rain,
The waterfall of countless grains.
Powerless unto their fate,
Descension bound to their own weight.
Gravity O! Gravity!
Time's vice against humanity.
Weak the blood within our veins,
And short the glory of our reign.
All of mankind is numbered,
And if one lives death won't slumber.
Man devoured without grace,
The final hour of our race.
Then before my bleeding eyes,
There came the moment of demise.
No more souls yet still to fall,
And no way from this dark to crawl.
Every soul in death entwined:
For time has run through all mankind.

**The Hourglass
Part II**

1
In the pit which none can climb,
On ragged rocks lay all mankind.
Faith in man now laid to waste,
Yet still in hopelessness I faced
Up to that window of light,
For some saviour to break the night.
Then, behold, was hope reborn,
There stood a man against the dawn.
How it was he hadn't fell
To this abyss I couldn't tell.
Surely human in his form,
Yet not to gravity conformed.
He was but material,
Yet somehow too celestial.
I watched that defiant grain,
The only one yet to be slain.
Man's last representative,
The last our species has to give:
The end of a broken line
Standing against the wrath of time.

The Hourglass
Part II

2
In the brightness stood above,
Blazing against the darkest flood,
Golden helm and javelin,
Clothed mankind's final paladin.
Valour in his purple threads,
His blood of power crimson red;
And reflecting in his eyes,
The stars roaming through endless skies.
Spear and sword was wielding,
With Alpha mark his shielding.
'Twas a sight of majesty,
This man shrouded in mystery.
By what strength does this man pass
That he defies the hourglass?
Surely some divinity,
Inside his veins since infancy,
On the edge where man was damned,
Was here Achilles made his stand.
Beating bronze upon his breast,
He called his foe to face it's death.

**The Hourglass
Part II**

3
In defence a beast arose:
Of pure hatred was composed.
Time itself made up its form,
A foe so twisted and deformed,
Writhing itself from the earth,
In hideous and fearsome birth.
Scales black his rancid cloak,
His veiled fangs of death invoke.
Serpent of dark majesty
Who watched the birth of gravity.
Rule over humanity:
In each scale a century.
Fangs injecting liquid death,
All hopelessness upon its breath.
Temptation calls from its eyes,
And in its mouth the birth of lies.
Here the hunter and the prey,
Their sword and venom on display.
Truly if Achilles fell,
Then man in time would ever dwell.

The Hourglass
Part II

4
Rain fell down and thunder cracked;
The beast leapt forth in fierce attack.
Their collision shook the world,
As sword and fang were beat and hurled.
Fierce the strikes that he unleashed,
Yet fast as lightening was the beast.
Flames from the abyss arose;
The beast rose up to striking pose.
In its eyes the rage insane
And fear that it would lose its reign.
Dark into the overhang,
Achilles fought the deadly fangs.
Yet the beast made deadly grip
With such a strength it did constrict.
Golden armour breaking in,
Achilles' strength forsaking him.
His departing breath of life,
Man's beating heart under the knife.
Caught inside the strangle hold,
Achilles veins were growing cold.

The Hourglass
Part II

5
From the coils of the snake,
Achilles cut and made escape.
Then upon the blood-soaked ground,
Achilles threw the serpent down.
Fear covered the serpent's face;
For him Achilles had no grace:
Crushing the snake underfoot,
Into the ashes and the soot.
Yet by fang his heel struck,
Achilles in the venom stuck.
To the ground fell heaven's sword,
The sands of time now fully poured.
Death took our deliverance,
As burning sun took Icarus.
His descent was like nightfall,
For darkness came and covered all.
Through the serpent had been slain,
Achilles died; our chains remain.
Although time has been destroyed,
This hourglass still owns the void.

The Hourglass
Part II

6
Into mourning man was cast,
For Sun into the shadows passed.
Death and silence covered all:
Achilles wasn't meant to fall.
There our saviour lay broken,
A celestial torn open.
Where two streams now trickled down,
Salvation now to death is bound.
Here the deepest tragedy,
That valour's veins could bleed empty.
Man of once eternal length,
By time slain in hideous strength.
In the chasm of dry bones,
Achilles lay in death enthroned.
An illusion was our hope;
A bitter gall which now we choke.
Violence was his death and pain;
In silence now he dwells in flame.
Soundlessness, I cannot stand
This silent planet lost to man.

**The Hourglass
Part II**

7
There Achilles lay condemned,
Surrounded by the bones of men;
And around encircling,
The serpent bones and dragon wings.
Crushed by the material,
The man who walked celestial.
Darkness closed in like a cloak,
Which covered all like darkest smoke.
All illumination ceased,
As death was dealt out by the beast.
All our light to absence passed,
As darkness filled the hourglass,
Eating light so greedily,
When I was naught but cecity.
Darkness more than just the night,
Is more than just absence of light.
Heart of darkness in us all,
That I so deeply knew its call.
For three cycles there I wept,
In sorrow such and sadness swept.

The Hourglass
Part II

8
Awful silent agony,
The cold and dark surrounding me.
Not my cries nor gazing eyes,
Made any sound or sight arise.
Screaming through my choking veins,
In blindness, deafness, rage and pain,
Suddenly there came a change:
A sound from silence was estranged.
As loud as a lightning crack,
A rhythm broke out through the black.
Sound not heard in centuries,
So stark was its intensity.
Sending silence reeling back,
Defeated beast into the black.
Here the sound of life did beat,
That now silence and death would meet.
Echoing through skeletons,
A sound laced with adrenaline.
That rhythm in perfect form,
Was a heartbeat of life now born.

The Hourglass
Part II

9
Silence in the sound defeat,
Yet still the cycle incomplete.
As I peered towards the place,
The rhythmic heartbeat picked up pace.
Darkness then was ripped apart,
As light burst outwards from the heart,
Blazing wonderous and white,
From darkness giving back our sight.
From the subtlety of sound,
The majesty of light unbound.
Light without impurity,
Now bringing forth transparency.
Colour from the white burst free,
The purple of the majesty.
Crimson red of blood once slain,
Again now beating through the veins.
Streams of light and colour flowed,
From in the heart where they were sowed.
Though that blinding light I gazed,
So deep into the flaming blazed.

The Hourglass
Part II

10
Even though light pained my eyes,
I looked, not caring if I died.
Gazing upward, all mankind,
All fears and hopes were now combined.
'Twas upon that hill of bones,
Of man's descent to the unknown.
There upon that sand dune high,
Achilles made his fall from sky.
There on top a silhouette,
The serpent's bones by light beset.
There behind that twisting spine,
A blaze behind the skull of time.
There the figure where light poured,
The wielder of heaven's sword.
Before whom the ground trembled,
The almighty elemental.
Truest form of Achilles,
Now clothed inside of majesty.
Could this be salvation's source?
The sword of heaven bound in force?

The Hourglass
Part II

11
He was bowed in steady breath,
The heart of light who tasted death.
Then he slowly raised his head,
Over the land of fallen dead;
Gazing out upon his kind,
Who shared with form but not decline.
Once was bound in mortal span,
Now bound celestial this man.
I was frozen in my fear
When he opened his eyes so clear.
Heat was his affinity,
As flames from him burst instantly.
So ferocious were the flames,
Too powerful to be contained.
Heat so incomparable,
So beautiful and terrible.
Fangs of time were laid to waste,
The venom vanquished and displaced.
Bones of snake cast to the void
Its wretched form was now destroyed.

The Hourglass
Part II

12
Here Achilles essence true,
In luminescence breaking through.
Still he spread the flames divine,
No ending here in wretched time,
But reforming bones from dust
And giving sinews back to us:
Weaving flesh upon our forms,
As skeletons made whole and warm.
Blindness from our eyes was torn,
And deafness broken by the dawn.
Here a star of sanctity,
Among fallen humanity.
Nature's laws turned inside out;
The very stones now stand and shout.
Sword of heaven now unleashed,
That cuts the earth so deep beneath.
Victory was still not won,
The hourglass still not undone.
Then Achilles raised his eyes
Towards the darkness of the skies.

The Hourglass
Part II

13
From his feet the whole ground fell,
The sea of sand began to swell.
Through the leverage of space,
All gravity had been displaced.
Bound in blazing flame ornate,
His frame began to levitate.
Icarus reborn in flames,
The heavens now his rightful claim.
Through space flight was not obtained,
For space itself he rearranged.
Measureless his majesty,
Untethered from the earth and sea.
Reign of gravity foreclosed,
The kingdom of Achilles rose.
Limitless in every sense,
As Hades fell without defence.
Bound inside of phoenix flames,
The skies are now his prize to claim.
Gate to life above his eyes;
To where man fell, I watched him rise.

The Hourglass
Part II

14
In his majesty so vast,
Ascending through the hourglass;
Up to life and death's portal,
The flight of heaven's immortal:
Then Achilles reached the place,
Where all mankind did fall from grace.
Bursting forth in awesome light,
Arisen from the darkest night,
Time in blood has been unmade,
The ransom of the reaper paid.
All of death and gravity,
Now swept aside by majesty.
Now the hourglass he owns,
Yet here Achilles made no throne.
Life and death now in his hand,
Yet still his feet arose from land.
His flight was immutable,
The hourglass immovable,
As the darkened skies eclipsed
By flames of the apocalypse.

The Hourglass
Part II

15
Momentum beyond my eyes,
Enough perhaps to shatter skies.
Fearing the oncoming death,
I drew and held the deepest breath.
Then Achilles made contact:
Earth shattering, the great impact.
Ripping the air from my lungs,
The cataclysm had begun.
Crashing at the great divide,
Eternity and time collide.
Shock waves forced me to the ground,
I lost all sense of sight and sound.
Deep vibrations shaking me,
Tempestuous was Hades' sea.
Up and down the hourglass,
A schism formed none could surpass.
Through tremors I raised my eyes,
To the collision in the skies.
There behold! the sky was torn,
As upwards was Achilles bourn.

The Hourglass
Part II

16
There a hole inside the glass,
A window to the ancient past,
Time no longer crowning reigns,
Prometheus now free of chains.
Now eternity in sight,
Yet still unreachable in height.
Then came thunder loud and hard
That tore the sky up into shards;
And the lightening followed fast
In cracks that filled the sky so vast.
From the hole Achilles made
The sky was slit by heaven's blade.
Spreading cracks like a disease,
The world was splintered with such ease:
Splinters of the sky so wide,
In the apocalyptic tide.
Timelessness consumed the past,
As fault lines took the hourglass.
Then in fear I realised
The cracks were spreading from the skies.

The Hourglass
Part II

17
Every soul from in the pit,
All saw as the horizon split
From the hole that pierced the arc,
The cracks of light that broke the dark.
Breaking down these dark confines,
To desolation all resigned,
Fear arose to see that hole,
And soon my mind had lost control.
Nothing I can do but gaze,
And then the sky began to cave.
To the earth the sky did crash,
In fear all men began to thrash.
Driving deep into the sand,
The shards of glass now cast and damned,
Anarchy began to fall
As I did flee to carven walls.
Then I reached the great divide,
Yet still from death I could not hide:
Hand on glass and beating heart,
As through my hands it tore apart.

The Hourglass
Part II

18
Here the end of every age,
The breaking down of man and cage.
Still bound to her gravity,
The earth she shook so frantically.
Soon the cracks below my feet
In the apocalypse would meet.
Every foundation would crack
And cast all men to light and black.
Chasms vast were opening,
Through population reckoning.
Merciless the motion bound,
Into the centre of the ground.
Driving to the mirror dark,
The cracks of doom closing their arcs.
Then, behold! the cracks did meet,
As shock waves threw me from my feet.
All the glass surrounding me,
Exploded into cosmic sea.
I was cast unwillingly
Into the black eternity.

The Hourglass
Part III

1
Sand like stars scattered the sky;
Eternity eclipsed my eyes.
Bound by beauty upward borne,
A stairway through the swirling storm.
Through time which had been transgressed,
A tunnel right through the tempest.
On the waves I upward passed,
My form transforming into glass,
Swirling through the great spiral
Of cosmic clouds now unbridled.
Then shot forth in timeless form,
I rose above the swirling storm.
Then with my once mortal eyes,
I saw the space beyond Earth's skies.
Yet the stars were not the same
That as a child I could name,
My countless constellations,
Forming freed of their foundations.
And beneath me was no ground,
From gravity I was unbound.

The Hourglass
Part III

2
Neither within nor outside,
But here where nebulas collide;
And the great wonder beheld,
That under time no longer held.
Second and a century,
Are now one and the same to me.
With my very soul in tune,
With every planet star and moon;
And throughout the universe,
Upon the waves of change traverse.
From the east Orion rose,
Of countless stars he was composed,
From his ancient orbit freed,
Now dancing through the endless sea:
Every move a symphony,
Each star a chord of symmetry.
Streaming stars in dance and flow,
Like leaves upon a wind did blow.
Floating through the cosmic clouds,
Majestic colour was his shroud.

The Hourglass
Part III

3
Stars which slid past me like snow,
Awash in heaven's deepest glow,
He looked up towards the west
And laid his bow at last to rest.
Here his last journey begins,
To further up and further in.
Then I heard a call from space,
Celestial restoring grace
Healing that once deadly curse,
As sending waves through universe.
And the path Orion laid
Was in his light: My way was made.
Then aside me Pluto rose,
Aglow in blue and yellow pose.
Keeping watch for centuries,
Were Pluto's eyes upon Hades.
But when I came through his clouds,
In new service he was endowed;
For Hades has slipped away,
Now lost in heavenly display.

The Hourglass
Part III

4
Leaving that horizon bright,
As dark of space began to light,
Neptune rising in the tune,
And I drawn in became a moon
Gazing down upon his sea,
A tempest-writhing agony.
In such force did waves collide,
Poseidon couldn't tame these tides.
Waters nothing could appease,
Yet then I felt the softest breeze.
Coming down it kissed the surge.
A tiny ripple there emerged
And at peace the sea became,
As tidal waves grew small and tame
To the softest touch of air,
To which the tides could not compare.
Shadows turned to aqua blue,
As murky shallows life imbued.
Neptune moving up in song,
Eternal tunes where he belongs.

The Hourglass
Part III

5
Then there rose an entity,
Ancient among the heavenly.
Swirling clouds of ice his skin,
The father of the Titan kin.
And, behold, I saw there rise,
A world of rings and golden skies.
Son and Father once in hate,
Yet love has made their way so straight.
Two planets rebound in peace,
Renewed by waves of sweet release.
Death and time are now no more,
So further up and in we draw.
Then rose one in purple shawl,
And one to him appeared so small.
Jupiter the almighty;
Beside him tiny Mercury.
Yet these stars they stand as one,
Their orbits now have been re-spun.
Now they bow to but one King
To whom we fly on westward wings.

The Hourglass
Part III

6
Then I saw most red of stars
Was the almighty soldier, Mars.
Visions filling up my mind,
Of all the war which man did bind.
Through my mind the arrows flew,
And smoke coloured the sky once blue.
Violent hands all peace defied,
And, followed by that silent cry,
There I stood upon that field
Of bodies strewn and splintered shield.
Great the sacrifice of man,
To die for lines drawn by his hands.
There alone among the dead,
The ground itself was bleeding red:
Blood as deep as wretched sea,
Now reasonless in memory.
Just another lovely war,
When time bound men upon her shores.
In the dark my head was bowed,
Until a light broke through the clouds.

The Hourglass
Part III

7
Unto me light broke in waves
Inside the peace Achilles gave.
Light and rain together bloomed;
New growth came healing all the wounds.
Unto flint transformed the flames,
The spear heads lost into the plain.
Unto where they found their form,
Has now returned under the morn.
Watching ancient swords grow rust,
Until they wore away to dust,
Yet still bravery remains,
Now purified in falling rain.
Now here in eternity,
From war mankind at last is free.
Then to me returned my eyes,
As Mars before me roamed the skies.
And behind his weapon lay,
For homeward is his final way:
Further up and free of war,
And further into heaven's store.

The Hourglass
Part III

8
Then arose a woman's form
Behind a veiling cosmic storm.
Sunlit clouds her silken thread,
Her atmosphere a satin bed.
And a thought in me arose
To pull the petals from the rose.
All her nectar dripping sweet,
Behind her clouds upon her sheet.
Moving slowly in her grace,
Until we stood there, face to face.
Yet within I felt the shame,
For I not even knew her name.
Sunlight gave me clarity
Upon this living tragedy.
The most wealthy prostitute,
In her own beauty destitute,
Was a loveless life of lust
That turned her beauty into dust.
From the siren dance I turned,
For loveless romance only spurns.

The Hourglass
Part III

9
Yet as light so filled her room,
Transforming faithless into bloom,
In her beauty figure dressed,
By westward grace her form was blessed.
Vulcan gone, now she is free,
Restored in heaven's purity.
All forgiven is her past,
In days of lust and hourglass.
Dancing innocence restored
To Mars who stood returned from war.
Once again, now side by side,
The soldier and his faithful bride
Under sky by colour stained,
They sang their vows in joyful strains.
From her eyes her veil slipped,
And tenderly Mars kissed her lips.
Then I saw a moon caressed,
There suckling on Venus' breast.
Love restored their family
From further in the galaxy.

The Hourglass
Part III

10
Following their wedding dance,
Through great and luminous expanse
Beauty so spectacular,
The colour flowing nebulas
Decorating heaven's heights,
As we were drawn to growing light.
Whereupon I saw, behold,
My home and world in sunlit gold.
Forming like a shooting star,
I had returned from so afar.
Oh! The joy that welled in me,
When I beheld my world was free.
With the hourglass no more,
So overturned was time and war
What was once material,
Now one with the celestial.
And I sang in joyful strains
To see my world now free of pain.
As my lyrics touched the earth,
My childhood lament reversed.

**The Hourglass
Part III**

11
Down through purple clouds I came
To see my home in healing rain,
Ancient desert turned to green
As meadows came and filled the scene.
There I saw the flowers bloom:
No more for winter to consume
Were the ravages of time,
That made the rose in thorns entwined.
Yet now every forest grows;
All drought and death no longer knows:
For the rains have come at last
To wash away the painful past.
Now in the eternal realm,
In harmony the pine and elm.
Once again will nature sing,
And gifts of fruit the trees will bring.
Blossoming in spring unfurled,
As flowers colouring the world.
Yet their nectar had no bees,
Nor any creature I could see.

The Hourglass
Part III

12
Through the woods my way was made,
And strayed to an enchanted glade.
There sat Pan in ancient sleep,
His form to stone by time did keep.
Then I watched the rising dawn
Bring light to wood and touch the fawn.
Light and song undid the curse,
His eyes awake in brand new verse.
Pan and pipe, he played a tune,
The hold of time on life was hewn.
Creatures out of slumber came,
Beyond number and called by name.
Giant beasts of ages past,
All broken free of fossil cast.
Every feather tusk and claw,
Forever freed from time's old law.
And Pan led them to their homes,
Through jungles, deserts, catacombs.
The undying seasons bloom,
The piper calling all to tune.

**The Hourglass
Part III**

13
Through Achilles' majesty,
The myriad of life set free.
Then all creatures upward gazed,
As greatest symphony was raised.
In the tongues of every bird,
And languages of every herd.
Sweet creation's song anew
In exaltation raised in tune.
And my spirit rose upon
My soul ascending in their song.
Like an eagle soaring through,
The creatures of the green and blue.
Leaving the earth's atmosphere,
Until I stood in heaven's spheres,
Floating in the symphony
Upon the waves of cosmic sea.
Earth once silent in descent,
Now sings the loudest in ascent.
Bound by grace one single kin,
Most further up and further in.

**The Hourglass
Part III**

14
Spiralling the heavenly
Now out of exile, truly free.
All around my form there moved,
Eternal colours now infused.
Massive clouds like curtains fell,
And there behind Almighty dwells.
There behind that coloured wall,
The blazing flames that made us all.
Then in two the clouds were torn,
The Sun broke forth in greatest dawn.
All creation looked away
From the unbearable display.
Blinding, burning, blazing bright:
No darkness to pollute the white.
Heat so incomparable,
The light so pure and terrible;
All of heaven's majesty,
All power and authority:
Space was shaken by the Light,
And cast unto the void was night.

The Hourglass
Part III

15
I fell down upon my knees,
For truly I was unworthy.
Surely wretched I must be,
Before the weight of majesty.
Downcast was my shameful face,
Deserving death in full embrace.
Blazing was the light that bloomed,
And yet my soul was not consumed.
Raising up, my listless eyes,
Accepting blindness, would incise.
Yet, behold, I was not burned,
As if a sunspot had been turned.
Peering deep into the light,
I found the shape that broke the white.
There, behold, was Achilles,
Whose shadow covered over me.
By his silhouette I'm saved
From the consuming solar waves:
My sunlit saviour glowing,
Cleaning his sword in light flowing,

The Hourglass
Part III

16
Then at last I understood,
How was the hourglass withstood.
For Achilles' human form,
To sand and star-dust both conformed.
Perfect sand faced gravity,
In all his cosmic majesty,
Now standing in victory
Between the Sun and galaxy.
And I knew that they were one,
Achilles and the blazing Sun.
Then around their woven shape,
Huge solar flares made their escape.
In cosmic waves of fire,
Sending out their blazing spires.
Raising men in flaming shroud,
As dancing through creation bowed.
The fire was the wave of change,
By which the stars were rearranged.
Now they touch the hearts of men,
Restoring them to peace again.

**The Hourglass
Part III**

17
There the Sun in radiance,
A glow circled his radius.
And in front the silhouette,
Achilles there in glory set.
Then at last my eyes could see,
The One Being, Three Entities.
Then I felt my pulse restart,
As cosmic glow lit up my heart.
Then I saw myself at last,
In all of my most twisted past.
In two natures I was born,
And my spirit was always torn.
My form was material,
Yet called to be celestial.
Thrice I had in weakness turned
From heaven's light which always burned.
In sorrow my spirit wept,
For into darkness I had crept.
Tears were falling through my hands
And dripping on a shore of sand.

The Hourglass
Part III

18
From the space below my feet,
The earth did rise as we did meet.
With me stood the line of man,
So stretching out a shore of sand
At the edge of endlessness
Of man's eternal genesis.
And now just one thing remains,
Of time and death and human pain.
Ancient as the hourglass,
The only freedom from our past.
Gifted by the Sun divine,
A single choice older than time.
And that choice that we all made,
Is now the fate to which we're laid.
True for all of humanity,
This choice defines eternity.
Two paths laid before my eyes,
In each a place of time's demise.
Two roads pave eternity:
One of flight; One of gravity.